Performance

Management

:: *Author* ::

GANESHBHAI C. NARBHAVAR

(M.COM., B.ED., G-SET)

PUBLISHED BY

The New Era International Publishing House
HQ. At & Po. Chaveli., Ta- Chansma,
Dist- Patan, North Gujarat, India, Asia.
www.iphouseindia.com

First Publication: 23rd NOVEMBER, 2015

ISBN:- *978-1-51747-700-4*

Price: Rs.800/- INDIA

$ 15 OUTSIDE INDIA

PUBLISHED BY

**The New Era International Publishing House
HQ. At & Po. Chaveli., Ta- Chansma,
Dist- Patan, North Gujarat, India, Asia.
www.iphouseindia.com**

Dedicated
to
my
Parents

Performance Management - Meaning, System and Process

Definition of Performance Management

The role of HR in the present scenario has undergone a sea change and its focus is on evolving such functional strategies which enable successful implementation of the major corporate strategies. In a way, HR and corporate strategies function in alignment. Today, HR works towards facilitating and improving the performance of the employees by building a conducive work environment and providing maximum opportunities to the employees for participating in organizational planning and decision making process.

Today, all the major activities of HR are driven towards development of high performance leaders and fostering employee motivation. So, it can be interpreted that the role of HR has evolved from merely an appraiser to a facilitator and an enabler.

Performance management is the current buzzword and is the need in the current times of cut throat competition and the organizational battle for leadership. *Performance management is a much broader and a complicated function of HR, as it encompasses activities such as joint goal setting, continuous progress review and frequent communication, feedback and coaching for improved performance, implementation of employee development programmes and rewarding achievements.*

The process of performance management starts with the joining of a new incumbent in a system and ends when an employee quits the organization.

Performance management can be regarded as a systematic process by which the overall performance of an organization can be improved by improving the performance of individuals within a team framework. It is a means for promoting superior performance by communicating expectations, defining roles within a required competence framework and establishing achievable benchmarks.

According to Armstrong and Baron (1998), Performance Management is both a strategic and an integrated approach to delivering successful results in organizations by improving the performance and developing the capabilities of teams and individuals.

The term performance management gained its popularity in early 1980's when <u>total quality management programs</u> received utmost importance for achievement of superior standards and quality performance. Tools such as job design, leadership development, training and reward system received an equal impetus along with the traditional performance appraisal process in the new comprehensive and a much wider framework. Performance management is an ongoing communication process which is carried between the supervisors and the employees through out the year. The process is very much cyclical and continuous in nature. A ***performance management system includes the following actions***.

- Developing clear job descriptions and employee performance plans which includes the key result areas (KRA') and performance indicators.

- Selection of right set of people by implementing an appropriate selection process.

- Negotiating requirements and performance standards for measuring the outcome and overall productivity against the predefined benchmarks.

- Providing continuous coaching and feedback during the period of delivery of performance.

- Identifying the training and development needs by measuring the outcomes achieved against the set standards and implementing effective development programs for improvement.

- Holding quarterly performance development discussions and evaluating employee performance on the basis of performance plans.

- Designing effective compensation and reward systems for recognizing those employees who excel in their jobs by achieving the set standards in accordance with the performance plans or rather exceed the performance benchmarks.

- Providing promotional/career development support and guidance to the employees.

- Performing exit interviews for understanding the cause of employee discontentment and thereafter exit from an organization.

A ***performance management process*** sets the platform for rewarding excellence by aligning individual employee accomplishments with the organization's mission and objectives and making the employee and the organization understand the importance of a specific job in realizing outcomes. By establishing clear performance expectations which includes results, actions and behaviors, it helps the employees in understanding what exactly is expected out of their jobs and setting of standards help in eliminating those jobs which are of no use any longer. Through regular feedback and coaching, it provides an advantage of diagnosing the problems at an early stage and taking corrective actions.

To conclude, performance management can be regarded as a proactive system of managing employee performance for driving the individuals and the organizations towards desired performance and results. It's about striking a harmonious alignment between individual and organizational objectives for accomplishment of excellence in performance.

Objectives of Performance Management

According to Lockett (1992), performance management aims at developing individuals with the required commitment and competencies for working towards the shared meaningful objectives within an organizational framework.

Performance management frameworks are designed with the objective of improving both individual and organizational performance by identifying performance requirements, providing regular feedback and assisting the employees in their career development.

Performance management aims at building a high performance culture for both the individuals and the teams so that they jointly take the responsibility of improving the business processes on a continuous basis and at the same time raise the competence bar by upgrading their own skills within a leadership framework. Its focus is on enabling goal clarity for making people do the right things in the right time. It may be said that the main objective of a performance management system is to achieve the capacity of the employees to the full potential in favor of both the employee and the organization, by defining the expectations in terms of roles, responsibilities and accountabilities, required competencies and the expected behaviors.

The main goal of performance management is to ensure that the organization as a system and its subsystems work together in an integrated fashion for accomplishing optimum results or outcomes.

The major *objectives of performance management* are discussed below:

- To enable the employees towards achievement of superior standards of work performance.
- To help the employees in identifying the knowledge and skills required for performing the job efficiently

as this would drive their focus towards performing the right task in the right way.

- Boosting the performance of the employees by encouraging employee empowerment, motivation and implementation of an effective reward mechanism.

- Promoting a two way system of communication between the supervisors and the employees for clarifying expectations about the roles and accountabilities, communicating the functional and organizational goals, providing a regular and a transparent feedback for improving employee performance and continuous coaching.

- Identifying the barriers to effective performance and resolving those barriers through constant monitoring, coaching and development interventions.

- Creating a basis for several administrative decisions strategic planning, succession planning, promotions and performance based payment.

- Promoting personal growth and advancement in the career of the employees by helping them in acquiring the desired knowledge and skills.

Some of the key concerns of a performance management system in an organization are:

- Concerned with the output (the results achieved), outcomes, processes required for reaching the results and also the inputs (knowledge, skills and attitudes).

- Concerned with measurement of results and review of progress in the achievement of set targets.

- Concerned with defining business plans in advance for shaping a successful future.

- Striving for continuous improvement and continuous development by creating a learning culture and an open system.

- Concerned with establishing a culture of trust and mutual understanding that fosters free flow of communication at all levels in matters such as clarification of expectations and sharing of information on the core values of an organization which binds the team together.

- Concerned with the provision of procedural fairness and transparency in the process of decision making.

The performance management approach has become an indispensable tool in the hands of the corporates as it ensures that the people uphold the corporate values and tread in the path of accomplishment of the ultimate corporate vision and mission. It is a forward looking process as it involves both the supervisor and also the employee in a process of joint planning and goal setting in the beginning of the year.

Evolution of Performance Management

The term performance management gained its importance from the times when the competitive pressures in the market place started rising and the organizations felt the need of introducing a comprehensive performance management process into their system for improving the overall productivity and performance effectiveness.

The *performance management process evolved in several phases*.

1. *First Phase:* The origin of performance management can be traced in the early 1960's when the performance appraisal systems were in practice.

During this period, ***Annual Confidential Reports (ACR's)*** which was also known as ***Employee service Records*** were maintained for controlling the behaviors of the employees and these reports provided substantial information on the performance of the employees.

Any negative comment or a remark in the ESR or ACR used to adversely affect the prospects of career growth of an employee. The assessments were usually done for ten traits on a five or a ten point rating scale basis. These traits were job knowledge, sincerity, dynamism, punctuality, leadership, loyalty, etc. The remarks of these reports were never communicated to the employees and strict confidentiality was maintained in the entire process. The employees used to remain in absolute darkness due to the absence of a transparent mechanism of feedback and communication. This system had suffered from many drawbacks.

2. ***Second Phase:*** This phase continued from late 1960's till early 1970's, and the key hallmark of this phase was that whatever adverse remarks were incorporated in the performance reports were communicated to the employees so that they could take corrective actions for overcoming such deficiencies. In this process of appraising the performance, the reviewing officer used to enjoy a discretionary power of overruling the ratings given by the reporting officer. The employees usually used to get a formal written communication on their identified areas of improvements if the rating for any specific trait used to be below 33%.

3. ***Third Phase:*** In this phase the term ACR was replaced by performance appraisal. One of the key changes that were introduced in this stage was that the employees were permitted to describe their accomplishments in the confidential performance reports. The employees were allowed to describe their accomplishments in the self appraisal forms in the end of a year. Besides inclusion of the traits in the

rating scale, several new components were considered by many organizations which could measure the productivity and performance of an employee in quantifiable terms such as targets achieved, etc. Certain organizations also introduced a new section on training needs in the appraisal form. However, the confidentiality element was still being maintained and the entire process continued to be control oriented instead of being development oriented.

4. *Fourth Phase:* This phase started in mid 1970's and its origin was in India as great business tycoons like Larsen & Toubro, followed by State Bank of India and many others introduced appreciable reforms in this field.

In this phase, the appraisal process was more development driven, target based (performance based), participative and open instead of being treated as a confidential process. The system focused on performance planning, review and development of an employee by following a methodical approach.

In the entire process, the appraisee (employee) and the reporting officer mutually decided upon the key result areas in the beginning of a year and reviewed it after every six months. In the review period various issues such as factors affecting the performance, training needs of an employee, newer targets and also the ratings were discussed with the appraisee in a collaborative environment.

This phase was a welcoming change in the area of performance management and many organizations introduced a new HR department for taking care of the developmental issues of the organization.

5. *Fifth Phase:* This phase was characterized by maturity in approach of handling people's issues. It was more performance driven and emphasis was on development, planning and improvement. Utmost importance was given to culture building, team appraisals and quality circles were established for assessing the improvement in the overall employee productivity.

The performance management system is still evolving and in the near future one may expect a far more objective and a transparent system.

Components of Performance Management System

Any effective performance management system includes the following components:

1. *Performance Planning:* Performance planning is the first crucial component of any performance management process which forms the basis of performance appraisals. Performance planning is jointly done by the appraisee and also the reviewee in the beginning of a performance session. During this period, the employees decide upon the targets and the key performance areas which can be performed over a year within the performance budget., which is finalized after a mutual agreement between the reporting officer and the employee.

2. *Performance Appraisal and Reviewing:* The appraisals are normally performed twice in a year in an organization in the form of mid reviews and

annual reviews which is held in the end of the financial year. In this process, the appraisee first offers the self filled up ratings in the self appraisal form and also describes his/her achievements over a period of time in quantifiable terms. After the self appraisal, the final ratings are provided by the appraiser for the quantifiable and measurable achievements of the employee being appraised. The entire process of review seeks an active participation of both the employee and the appraiser for analyzing the causes of loopholes in the performance and how it can be overcome. This has been discussed in the performance feedback section.

3. ***Feedback on the Performance followed by personal counseling and performance facilitation:*** Feedback and counseling is given a lot of importance in the performance management process. This is the stage in which the employee acquires awareness from the appraiser about the areas of improvements and also information on whether the employee is contributing the expected levels of performance or not. The

employee receives an open and a very transparent feedback and along with this the training and development needs of the employee is also identified. The appraiser adopts all the possible steps to ensure that the employee meets the expected outcomes for an organization through effective personal counseling and guidance, mentoring and representing the employee in training programmes which develop the competencies and improve the overall productivity.

4. *Rewarding good performance:* This is a very vital component as it will determine the work motivation of an employee. During this stage, an employee is publicly recognized for good performance and is rewarded. This stage is very sensitive for an employee as this may have a direct influence on the self esteem and achievement orientation. Any contributions duly recognized by an organization helps an employee in coping up with the failures successfully and satisfies the need for affection.

5. *Performance Improvement Plans:* In this stage, fresh set of goals are established for an employee and

new deadline is provided for accomplishing those objectives. The employee is clearly communicated about the areas in which the employee is expected to improve and a stipulated deadline is also assigned within which the employee must show this improvement. This plan is jointly developed by the appraisee and the appraiser and is mutually approved.

6. *Potential Appraisal:* Potential appraisal forms a basis for both lateral and vertical movement of employees. By implementing competency mapping and various assessment techniques, potential appraisal is performed. Potential appraisal provides crucial inputs for succession planning and job rotation.

Need for an Effective Performance Management System

In the era of cut throat competition and globalization, organizations have realized the importance of strategic HR practices for gaining a competitive edge over the competitors. A well designed performance management system can play a crucial role in streamlining the activities of the employees in an organization for realizing the ultimate corporate mission and vision. Performance management is a useful tool for aligning all the major organizational functions and sub functions so that the focus is directed towards attainment of the organizational goal.

Performance management is a much broader system as it is linked with the processes of planning, implementing, reviewing and evaluating, for augmenting growth and productivity at both the individual and organizational level.

By clearly defining both individual and team based responsibilities in the form of KRA's as well as by creating an understanding of shared mutual accountabilities, a good performance management system enables, empowers and facilitates the development of staff members.

Managing the performance of the employees is one of the toughest challenges which the organizations are facing today as this completely depends upon the employee's commitment, competence and clarity of performance. If managed efficiently through a well planned reward practice and feedback mechanism, a performance management system can serve as an important tool for employee motivation and development. The need for the introduction of a robust system of performance management was felt during the period when the traditional performance appraisal mechanism started failing and its limitations were surfacing up. The performance appraisal system of the earlier period was missing objectivity as the diameters or the parameters for measuring performance were not clearly specified and the focus was on traits instead on behaviors or measurable targets. As a result, the employee's morale and motivation to work was adversely affected due to an absence of a transparent feedback mechanism and lack of employee involvement in the entire process of appraisal. A performance management system overcomes the drawbacks of the traditional performance appraisal system by maintaining a futuristic approach instead of assessing the past contributions of the employees for evaluating the performance of the employees.

Performance management is a strategic tool and is holistic in nature as it pervades in every activity of the organization which is concerned with the management of individual, team and the overall organizational performance. The process is indispensable and very important for an organization as it is concerned with establishing a culture in which the individuals and teams can excel by continuously improving in terms of skill sets and the business processes.

Performance management facilitates improvement of quality of relationship amongst the members of the organization by encouraging sharing of expectations and building a climate of openness and mutuality. The significance of performance management has grown in recent times because most of the organizations are giving a lot of importance to employee development and talent management. The contemporary organizations are working towards grooming the competencies of the employees for maintaining a leadership in the competitive market and performing outstandingly. Arvind Mills of Lalbhai Group, realized the importance of strategic HRM practices and the implementation of a pro active performance management system in their organization after facing serious threats from the business competitors. The company created a *Manpower Planning and Resource Group* which took the charge of preparing job descriptions and structuring the jobs for the employees and was responsible for implementing the recruitment and selection procedures. An innovative online recruitment system was introduced which was known as *Selection Information System*, for fixing interviews, generating call letters, etc. This system was linked with the *Compensation Information System* and *Training Information System*. The training requirements of the employees were taken care by the Management and Organizational Development Group. The company also introduced MBO system, for setting smart goals for the employees which may motivate them for a superior performance.

Performance management has attracted the attention of many organizations and in the near future its importance will still grow as it will become more integrated with the processes like talent management, career management, pay based on performance, development and talent management.

Performance Appraisal and Performance Management

The contemporary organizations are undergoing a transformation for coping against the changing needs of the environment and excelling in the business by building up their adaptive capabilities for managing change proactively. The traditional performance appraisal system did not suffice the needs of the changing scenario as it was mainly used as a tool for employee evaluation in which the managers were impelled to make subjective judgments about the performance and behavior of the employees against the predetermined job standards.

The main objective of the performance appraisal system was to exercise control over the activities of the employees through disciplinary actions and management of rewards and promotions. The supervisors were expected to rate their employees on certain traits ranging between a scale of unsatisfactory to outstanding performance and these ratings were susceptible to various errors like central tendency, bias, halo effect, etc.

Performance appraisals were mostly carried out annually for measuring the degree of accomplishment of an individual and were implemented on a top down basis in which the supervisors had a major role to play in judging the performance of an employee without soliciting active involvement of the employee. Performance appraisals were mostly discredited because it was backward looking concentrating largely on the employee's inabilities and flaws over a period of a year instead of looking forward by identifying the development needs of the employees and improving them. Traditionally, the performance appraisals were organized in a bureaucratic manner and suffered from unnecessary delays in decisions and corruption. Performance appraisals were mostly narrowly focused and functioned in isolation without bearing any linkage with the overall organizational vision or goals. The side effects of the performance appraisal system was it generated skepticism amongst the managers and the employees on any new initiative of the HR.

In the present scenario, the organizations have shifted their focus from performance appraisals to performance management as a result of internationalization of human resources and globalization of business. The functions of HRM have become far more complicated as today the major focus of strategic HRM practices is on the management of talent by implementing such development programmes which enhance the competencies of the employees. The performance management approach focuses more on observed behaviors and concrete results based on the previously established smart objectives. By adopting techniques like Management by Objectives (MBO), smart objectives are established in terms of either facts and figures and in the entire process the superior plays the role of a coach or a facilitator. The objectives are mutually decided at the beginning of the performance season and serve as a standard of performance for evaluation. In this method, the employees can offer a feedback on their contributions by filling up a self appraisal form. Performance management is a much broader term in comparison with performance appraisal as it deals with a gamut of activities which performance appraisals never deal with. This system is a strategic and an integrated approach which aims at building successful organizations by developing high performance teams and individuals and improving the performance of people. This process starts when a job is defined. Performance management emphasizes on front end planning instead of looking backward unlike performance appraisals and the focus is on ongoing dialogue instead of appraisal documents and ratings. Thus, performance management may be regarded as a continuous process.

A table depicted below shows a comparison between performance appraisal and performance management:

Performance Appraisal	*Performance Management*
Focus is on top down assessment	Stresses on mutual objective setting through a process of joint dialogue

Performed annually	Continuous reviews are performed
Usage of ratings is very common	Usage of ratings is less common
Focus is on traits	Focus is on quantifiable objectives, values and behaviors
Monolithic system	Flexible system
Are very much linked with pay	Is not directly linked with pay

Performance management is concerned with assumptions, mutual obligations, expectations and promises (Guest, D E et al, 1996). The views of some of the leading organizations of performance management approach are given below:

- According to Eli Lilly and Co., performance management focuses on aligning the individual goals with the goals of the organization and ensures that the employees work on the right tasks and do the right things.

- According to Standard Chartered Bank, performance management is concerned with those processes and behaviors by way of which the managers manage the performance of the employees for developing high achieving organizations.

Benefits of a Performance Management System

A good performance management system works towards the improvement of the overall organizational performance by managing the performances of teams and individuals for ensuring the achievement of the overall organizational ambitions and goals. *An effective performance management system can play a very crucial role in managing the performance in an organization by:*

- Ensuring that the employees understand the importance of their contributions to the organizational goals and objectives.

- Ensuring each employee understands what is expected from them and equally ascertaining whether the employees possess the required skills and support for fulfilling such expectations.

- Ensuring proper aligning or linking of objectives and facilitating effective communication throughout the organization.

- Facilitating a cordial and a harmonious relationship between an individual employee and the line manager based on trust and empowerment.

Performance management practices can have a positive influence on the job satisfaction and employee loyalty by:

- Regularly providing open and transparent job feedbacks to the employees.

- Establishing a clear linkage between performance and compensation

- Providing ample learning and development opportunities by representing the employees in leadership development programmes, etc.

- Evaluating performance and distributing incentives and rewards on a fair and equated basis.
- Establishing clear performance objectives by facilitating an open communication and a joint dialogue.
- Recognizing and rewarding good performance in an organization.
- Providing maximum opportunities for career growth.

An effectively implemented performance management system can benefit the organization, managers and employees in several ways as depicted in the table given below:

Organization's Benefits	Improved organizational performance, employee retention and loyalty, improved productivity, overcoming the barriers to communication, clear accountabilities, and cost advantages.
Manager's Benefits	Saves time and reduces conflicts, ensures efficiency and consistency in

	performance.
Employee's Benefits	Clarifies expectations of the employees, self assessment opportunities clarifies the job accountabilities and contributes to improved performance, clearly defines career paths and promotes job satisfaction.

Clearly defined goals, regular assessments of individual performance and the company wide requirements can be helpful in defining the corporate competencies and the major skill gaps which may in turn serve as a useful input for designing the training and development plans for the employees. A sound performance management system can serve two crucial objectives:

Evaluation Objectives

- By evaluating the readiness of the employees for taking up higher responsibilities.
- By providing a feedback to the employees on their current competencies and the need for improvement.

- By linking the performance with scope of promotions, incentives, rewards and career development.

Developmental Objectives

The developmental objective is fulfilled by defining the training requirements of the employees based on the results of the reviews and diagnosis of the individual and organizational competencies. Coaching and counseling helps in winning the confidence of the employees and in improving their performance, besides strengthening the relationship between the superior and the subordinate.

In a nutshell, performance management serves as an important tool for realizing organizational goals by implementing competitive HRM strategies. It helps in aligning and integrating the objectives with the KPI's in an organization both vertically and horizontally across all job categories and the levels and thus helps in driving all the activities right from the bottom level towards one single goal.

Prerequisites for a Performance Management System

Performance management can be regarded as a continuous process managing the performances of people for getting desired results. Performance management is beneficial to all the major stakeholders of an organization by clearly describing what is supposed to be done for attaining certain desired goals. Performance management is the heart of any HR processes in an organization as it influences the rest other HR functions or processes. Focus on performance management may be fruitless without the existence of proper organizational design and management systems.

Some of the essential pre requisites without which performance management system will not function effectively in an organization are:

- Should attract very high levels of participation from all the members concerned in an organization. It should be a participative process.
- Top management support and commitment is very essential for building a sound performance culture in an organization.

- Organizational vision, mission and goals should be clearly defined and understood by all levels so that the efforts are directed towards the realization of the organizational ambitions.

- Clear definition of the roles for performing a given job within the organizational framework which emanates from the departmental and the organizational objectives. The system should also be able to explain the linkages of a role with other roles.

- Open and transparent communication should prevail which will motivate the employees for participating freely and delivering high performance. Communication is an essential pre requisite for a performance management process as it clarifies the expectations and enables the parties in understanding the desired behaviors or expected results.

- Identification of major performance parameters and definition of key performance indicators.

- Consistency and fairness in application.

- A commitment towards recognition of high performance. Rewards and recognitions should be built within the framework of performance management framework.

. Proper organizational training should be provided to the staff members based on the identification of training needs from periodic evaluation and review of performance. This will motivate the employees for a superior performance.

Tata Iron and Steel Company (TISCO), a flagship company of India involved in manufacturing of cost effective steel can be appreciated for their initiatives in the implementation of an effective performance management framework and innovative HR practices. TISCO initiated a management restructuring programme for transforming into a high performing and a growing organization. In the HR front, the management focused on providing exciting career opportunities and building a team of high performing professionals for which they hired Mckinsey and Co. The consultants firstly started with building a lean and a flat strategic business unit with enriched jobs, increased accountabilities and autonomy. A Performance Ethic Programme (PEP) was also introduced for promoting young and dynamic professionals and this was a replacement of seniority based promotions. A new Performance Management System (PMS) was introduced for aligning the KRA's with the business strategies and identifying superior performers in the organization by defining clear career paths and accountabilities. The rewards and recognitions were linked with the PMS. The new measures in the direction of performance management boosted the employee's motivation and performance. The job satisfaction also improved due to the introduction of a fair and transparent reward system.

Stages in the Development and Implementation of a Performance Management System

Performance management is a strategic process and an integrated approach. The process involves an ongoing dialogue between the supervisor and the employee for setting goals which are achievable and contribute in the direction of fulfillment of the organizational goal. The main objective of performance management approach is to proactively manage employee's performance for accomplishing organizational goals by attaining a desired level of performance. It believes in linking the performance plans of an organization with the strategic vision and identifying the major performance indicators and KRA's for enabling the employees to achieve the expected outcomes for their organization.

Any performance management process broadly involves three stages and these are:

1. *Goal Setting and Motivation* which is normally done in the beginning of the session.
2. *Encouraging Stage* which is normally undertaken when the employees get involved in the process of pursuit of the assigned task.
3. The final stage is the *Stage of Rewards and Consequences* which is applied after the completion of a task.

Performance management is always a forward planning process which is developmental and facilitative in nature as it involves the team leaders and the employees in a joint process of decision making for fixing smart targets.

It aims at breeding performance orientation in the employees for developing high performance organizations. The entire process involves identification, evaluation and development of the work performance of the employees through effective management practices like continuous coaching, feedback and regular communication. The process includes the following stages:

- Work Planning and defining expectations
- Monitoring performance
- Developing the weak performance areas
- Performance rating
- Rewarding good performance

Performance Management Process in Action Aid

The performance management system of Action Aid aims at continuous development of the staff members and recognizing their contributions, assessing the future potential and also the development needs which may be professional as well as personal and facilitating a shared understanding of mutual accountability through giving and receiving feedback. In Action Aid 360 degree feedback is performed which means feedback is elicited from multiple sources on key performance areas of the employees which are competency, behavior and attitude, values, work life balance, major achievements and areas of improvements. The performance management process in Action Aid passes through the following stages:

1. Identification of the Key Result areas both at the organizational level and the regional/unit level.

2. The staff members settle their work plans which are derived from the KRA's in the departmental level and also from the framework of their job descriptions. These work plans are laid down each year for the following year.

3. After defining the work plans, the staff members describe the key performance indicators which may also include some qualitative dimensions which can be measured in quantifiable terms and ultimately form the basis of assessment for the appraiser.

4. Identification of those set of behaviors and attitudes which are critical for effective performance.

5. Annual review of performance of the staff members against the plans and the behavioral dimensions which is done in a structured format and also the mid reviews are performed at the regional or the departmental level.

6. Identification of training needs of the staff members followed by finalization of a new action plan for the ensuing year.

In Action Aid, performance development is treated as a continuous process and a lot of importance is given to the feedback mechanism.

Competency Management Approach for Setting Superior Performance Benchmarks

In the present business environment of cut throat competition and globalization, competency based practices have gained much of an attention from the contemporary organizations. They aim at achieving an optimum performance in the long term by developing the skills and competencies of the employees on a continuous basis. *Competency based management systems are primarily employee centric performance management systems and focuses upon how an organization achieves a desired performance.* By aligning competencies within the performance management framework, the supervisors provide a feedback to the employees on the performance goals achieved and how the work was performed.

Competency focused performance management systems can serve as a useful tool for helping the employees in understanding the performance expectations and improving the competencies. Competency based management are strategic in nature and influences almost every area of human capital management which starts with the hiring of an employee and ends with the retirement. It aims at standardizing and integrating all HR activities by relying upon competencies which support fulfillment of organizational goals.

For example, *Maruti Udyog Limited* which was a joint venture with *Suzuki* of Japan realized the need of aligning HR strategies with the corporate strategies by linking competency mapping with the major systems of HR.

Deregulation in India in 1998 drastically declined the market share of Maruti which was earlier the undisputed leader in the automobiles industry. Reforms like competency mapping, job rotations, improvements in the appraisal system, initiatives in implementation of a transparent system of feedback and communication, clear definition of job profiles and their accountabilities and many others, improved the competitiveness of Maruti.

Performance management systems are based on personal competencies which distinguish high performers from the average performers and the personal competencies are derived from the values and core competencies of an organization (Reagan, 1994). According to Collins and Porras (1996), organizations which use core competencies based systems are regarded as high performers or visionaries. Competencies are primarily job specifications concerned with the knowledge, skills and abilities of an individual which defines the personal as well as the organizational success (Englemann & Roesch, 1996). The same researchers listed personal competencies as achievement orientation, team work, analytical thinking, relationship building, customer service orientation, etc. Individual competencies drive excellence in an organization as they are utilized as a yardstick for evaluating and monitoring both individual and organizational performance and their effectiveness (Antonacopoulou & FitzGerald, 1996).

Competencies can be integrated with the performance management process by any of the two ways:

1. ***By identifying and defining the key competencies required for realizing the performance goals/objectives:*** The key competencies are jointly defined by the manager and the employee during the stage of setting performance plans, goals and objectives. These competencies are ultimately assessed during the performance review period in connection with the performance goals/objectives realized by the employees.

2. ***By identifying the competencies which are required for performing an employee's job/role into the performance management process:*** In the case, the

competencies are identified from the competency profile from the employee's role or job point of view and also include the performance goals/objectives for being reviewed. The performance goals/objectives deal with the aspect of what must be achieved over the entire period of review and the competencies address the question of how an employee achieved the pre determined performance goal by demonstrating an expected pattern of behavior.

Competencies are aligned in each phase of the performance management cycle. CPS Human Resource Services has designed a model on Strategic Performance Management which is given below:

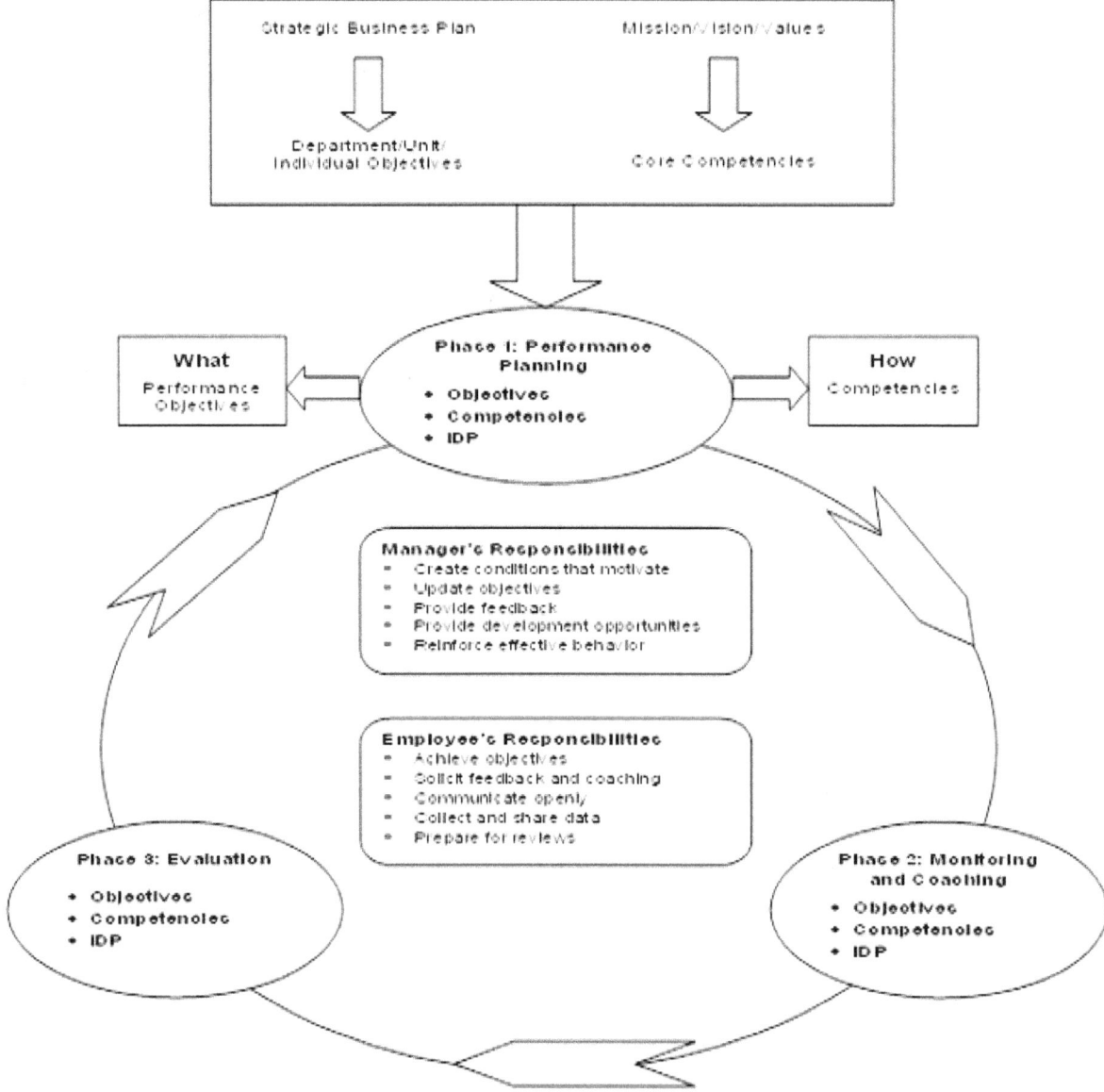

CPS Human Resource Services treats the process of performance management as a gap closing strategy, which focuses upon the vision, mission and values of the organization, the goals and objectives of the agency, individual goals and objectives and also the core competencies.

Organizations like ***Wipro and Infosys***, the major IT giants of India give a lot of importance to competency based performance management system. In Wipro, the performance management process begins with the identification and assessment of critical competencies for top management, senior management and middle management on the basis of critical incidents, focus groups and rigorous interviews. 360 degree feedback is used for providing a feedback on the existing competencies of the employees and based on the results of the feedback a training programme is organized for improving the deficit areas of performance. Finally, personal development plans are formulated for each employee for monitoring and tracking the improvement in competencies or skill sets. For building competencies, Wipro focuses on strategic thinking, vision, building star performers and global focus. Infosys equally gives a lot of importance to 360 degree feedback for evaluating the critical leadership competencies of their employees.

Talent Management Practices and Corporate Strategies

Organizations which wish to attract the best of talents and retain employees across all levels must have an integrated approach to talent management. According to latest survey findings from *Accenture High Performance Report*, about 85% senior executives view talent management as a major competitive differentiator for attracting and retaining skilled workforce and developing the highly talented leaders. Many Indian organizations have realized that it is the quality of people which they employ, retain and develop will ensure their business profitability and provide them a competitive advantage. Talent management is concerned with delivering business success by understanding what an organization actually means by talent and how it can achieve the long term organizational goals. It aims at ensuring that the organizations value natural talents and understand the obstructions to an effective performance.

Talent management solution integrates the needs of the management, executives and employees into one system and unifies information across all the major HR processes like performance management, recruitment and selection, learning and development, succession planning and career development. According to a survey report of *May 2006 from the Economist Intelligence Unit (EIU) and Development Dimensions International (DDI)*, maximum CEO's from across different industries globally spend their major chunk of time in recruiting, performance management, talent management, succession planning, mentoring and retention.

Talent management strategies are holistic in nature and aim at supporting such practices which improve the communication of goals and performance expectations across different levels in an organization. These strategies can be categorized into the following heads:

- Developing the existing talent pool
- Maximizing employee satisfaction
- Attracting talent visibility
- Planning in advance for succession
- Acting upon the performance reviewed

According to a report from *CIPD's 2006 learning and development survey*, managing talent is not a very easy job and various factors influence the talent management strategies and policies of an organization. The report equally highlights that about 74% of the respondents did not have a properly conceived plan for management of talent. Some of the major strategic challenges to talent management are:

- A rise in the trends of globalization in the labor market.
- An increase in the virtual workplaces.
- Diverse workforce in terms of age, race, etc.
- Educated workforce carries independent notions about their style of work and career path.

However, for many organizations talent management is a major strategic issue and they view it as a critical factor for providing them with a competitive advantage in the competitive war for talent. Effective management of talent requires a thorough diagnosis of the employee attitudes and also the organizational culture. The tools which help in attracting and retaining the best of talent in an organization are pay, benefits, learning and development and a proper work environment which can be group centric or individual and the benefits can be tangible or intangible.

Pay: This is the most determining factor for retaining the talent pool in an organization which should be kept competitive. IT and ITES majors like *Wipro and Infosys* implement variable pay for retaining the employees and extracting the best performance from them. Flexible benefits are another effective tool for encouraging high performers for example *Eicher Group* which allows its employees to design their own compensation package which suits with their needs.

Benefits: Benefits which provide social and futuristic security to the employees can serve as a major tool for retaining the best talent pool in an organization. For example, Infosys provides a group insurance scheme to its 13,000 employees in Bangalore and is also one of the first Indian software companies for introducing Employee Stock Option Plans (ESOP). Similarly, many other Indian organizations design and develop innovative benefit packages for retaining their talent.

Learning and Development: It enables the retention of the most competent and ambitious employees in the organization and at the same time provide a competitive advantage by building the intellectual base in an organization. For example, Wipro provides ample learning opportunities to its employees for developing their leadership potential. Wipro has designed a *Life Cycle Stage Development programme*, which selects the employees with the leadership potential and trains them in accordance with their level in the organization.

Organizational Culture: A healthy work environment boosts the morale and spirit of the employee and strengthens the bond of relationship between the management and the employees. Work culture is influenced by the organizational communication system, feedback mechanism and the effective implementation of recognition and rewards. Many Indian organizations have taken innovative initiatives for maximizing employee satisfaction and improving the overall organizational productivity.

Objective Setting and MBO-SMART Objectives

Defining the performance objectives can be very useful as it defines the performance expectations. Objectives which are written down and are verifiable can be far more useful if they are **SMART** in nature which means **Specific, Measurable, Achievable, Realistic and Time Bound**. Many organizations set goals and objectives through a formal process known as **Management by Objectives (MBO)** which is an organized and a systematic approach of defining organizational goals and realizing them within the available resources. The main aim of this approach is to improve organizational performance by aligning the organizational goals with the individual objectives at all levels and attaining those goals within a prescribed time frame. The system involves continuous monitoring and feedback for improving the quality of outcome.

The chief proponent of MBO system was Peter F Drucker in 1954 in his book entitled 'The Practice of management'. GE was the first organization to adopt the MBO method for defining goals. The major focus of this approach is on inviting participation from all the managers in the goal setting process and strategic planning and implementing a range of performance systems which help an organization to remain on the right path. On the whole, it may be regarded that objective setting process is an important part of performance management process as it defines and manages expectations by establishing an understanding on the part of the role holder about what has to be achieved and at the same time acts as a point of reference during the period of performance review.

Objectives can be broadly classified under the following heads:

1. ***Work Objectives:*** These are the key result areas in a role profile of an employee which not only explains what has to be done but also why a job has to be done. For example, respond proactively to the customer complaints and queries for maximizing

customer satisfaction. Effective work objectives clearly define an activity in terms of the results or standards which are to be accomplished. For example, Tata Steel for transforming itself into a growth organization aligns the key result areas with the corporate strategy at all levels in its performance management module. The organization rewards and provides career growth opportunities to those employees who perform well in their jobs. In this way the organization manages the performance of its employees by focusing on work objectives or the KRA's.

2. *Targets:* These are the results which can be measured in quantifiable terms like output, income, cost reduction, service delivered, etc.

3. *Tasks/Projects:* These are the objectives which carry a deadline and should be fulfilled within a specified time frame or can be completed in phases.

4. *Behavioral Parameters:* Behavioral parameters are normally set out within the competency frameworks, identified as desirable and undesirable behaviors

which may be useful in the process of performance planning and reviewing. For example, Infosys emphasizes on recruiting only those candidates who display a high degree of learnability and at the same time possess special competencies like analytical skills, communication skills and problem solving skills.

5. *Values:* The objective may be to drive all the efforts of the employees and the management team for up holding the core values of the company. In FedEx, the organization espouses the value of maximizing employee satisfaction for promoting customer satisfaction.

6. *Performance Improvement:* This objective aims at realization of an improved performance by directing all the attention towards achieving better results. This objective is highlighted in the performance improvement plans of the employees which describe what steps or measures can be jointly adopted by the managers and the employee for an optimal performance. South West Airlines aims at improving

the performance of its employees by providing them appropriate training for handling the requirements of the job challenges, compensating them favorably and keeping them motivated for winning their loyalty.

7. ***Developmental Objectives:*** These objectives are highlighted in the personal development plans and include the diverse areas of development for an employee which can help in the enhancement of skills and knowledge levels of an employee. In GE, training and development is a continuous process for developing the competencies of the employees and invests in both in-house training programmes and development programmes. Besides this, the company also sponsors its employees for MBA course in reputed universities.

Prerequisites for a good objective

- A good objective should be precise and well defined.
- Should be consistent with the values of an organization.

- Must fulfill the measurability criterion in quantifiable terms.

- Should be challenging for encouraging better performance and attainment of superior standards.

- Should be achievable and must be within the purview of an individual's capability.

- Should be mutually agreed by the manager and the employee concerned.

- Must be time bound and emphasize on team based results.

Techniques for Assessment of Performance and the Factors Affecting Assessments

A performance management process involves an assessment or an analysis of what has been achieved and forms a basis for career planning, potential development, performance agreements and development plans like **Douglas Mc. Gregor** suggested that emphasis should be on analysis and not on appraisal. Perfo rmance management process is forward looking. Performance assessments depend upon the ability to judge a performance which further depends upon specification of clear standards and avoidance of unnecessary projections. Perfect assessments can never completely be a reality and is susceptible to various errors or problems like halo effect which means the manager acquires a tendency of generalizing few experiences with the other aspects of performance and the problems of poor perception, selectivity and poor interpretation. For overcoming these problems the following remedial measures can be adopted:

- Ensuring that all the managers and employees understand the concept of performance and learn to differentiate between good performances with not so good ones.
- Encouraging managers to define and agree upon the standards and establishing different measures of effectiveness.
- Training managers to base their assessments and judgments after carefully scrutinizing the relevant data.

The different techniques which may be adopted for assessing the performance of employees in an organization are:

1. *A holistic analysis of performance:* The proponents of this approach believe that performance management is all about analyzing performance instead of assessing it. This technique aims at reaching an agreement for future action or development after carefully analyzing the strengths or possible weaknesses. Few organizations like BP Amoco implement this method of performance assessment for providing a feedback to the staff where they are good at.

2. *Narrative Assessment:* This is in the form of a written summary of views about different levels of performance achieved and is normally prepared by the managers. This technique lacks consistency in the criterion used for assessments as different managers will consider different aspects of performance.

3. *Ratings:* Many organizations like ICICI Bank and GE use ratings for assessing the performance of their

employees for making pay related decisions. Through this method the quality of performance or the competence level achieved by an employee in a particular skill can be assessed by evaluating it on a scale against certain parameters which may be qualitative (behavioral) or quantitative. Since, performance is a subjective concept; it is difficult to achieve consistency in the ratings which are offered by different managers. Regular trainings and peer reviews may help in promoting consistency in the ratings.

4. *Forced Distribution:* In this method, the manager is forced to offer his ratings according to the pattern of a normal curve. This technique rests on the basic assumption that the employees' performance levels fall under a normal statistical distribution.

5. *Forced Ranking:* In this method the employees are assigned ranking on the basis of categories. Since the concept of performance is vague so the rankings should be accompanied by meaningful performance data.

6. *Quota Systems:* Quota system specifies the distribution of ratings and accordingly adjusts the ratings of managers after an event for ensuring that the quota in each level is met.

Performance assessment is a very crucial yet a very difficult process. A combination of various assessment methods can yield good results.

Role of Managers in Performance Management

The success of performance management practices in any organization depend upon the commitment and involvement of the different stakeholders like top management, line managers, employees and the HR specialists.

Role of Top Managers in Performance Management

The top managers play a lead in the entire process by setting trends for the lower rung and acting as role models for the employees. Their responsibility is to design policies which ensure an efficient management of performance in an organization and to define and act upon the core values relating to performance. Top management plays a vital role in convincing the line managers that performance management can be instrumental in the achievement of business goals and thus ensure that they take this aspect seriously in their work front for maximizing employee satisfaction and productivity.

Top managers are expected to develop a high performance culture in an organization by ensuring the following:

- By communicating an organization's mission and values to its customers and employees.

- By clearly defining the work expectations and communicating to everyone for ensuring success in the achievement of business goals and facilitating an overall performance improvement.

- By keeping the employees informed about their progress towards the achievement of goals and suggesting corrective actions for non-achievement of performance.

- By establishing a shared belief amongst the employees regarding the importance of continuous improvement in performance.

A remarkable example is Infosys Technology Ltd., an international IT company and a world leader. The chairman Mr. Narayan Murthy was dedicated and committed towards an efficient management of performance of the employees for developing a vast talent pool in the organization. He considered his employees as the most powerful wealth responsible for driving the success and the future of his organization. He introduced the best reward systems in the industry for retaining the existing talent and the attracting the best from the industry. He encouraged an open communication and provided them with an opportunity to interact with the management and share ideas in meetings. He established a Leadership Institute in Mysore for grooming the future leaders for successfully tackling the challenges of the changing markets. Similary, the management of United Parcel Service of America (UPS), selects only those people who fit into their organizational culture for efficiently managing their performance and projecting a positive image before the customers.

Role of Line Managers in Performance Management

The line managers or the front line management play a very crucial role in implementing and enacting the HR policies. Hence, it is very important for the management to ensure that the line managers possess a right attitude towards the performance management approaches and equally possess the right competencies for executing it. The line managers mostly consider the performance management process as a mere bureaucratic chore and hence they consider it as a sheer waste of time. Some managers lack the required skills for reviewing the performance of the employees, providing feedback and identifying objectives along with them. These limitations can be overcome by adopting the following remedies:

- By providing leadership from the top.
- By communicating with the line managers about the importance of performance management in driving

successful results and how it is a part of their responsibility.

- By maintaining simplicity in the overall process of performance management.

- By reducing the pressure from the line managers by making the process an ongoing one instead of an annual review.

- By involving the line managers in the design and development of the performance management processes by representing them in pilot studies.

Role of Employees in Performance Management

The employees have a vital role to play in the performance management cycle as the entire process revolves around them. They play an active part in formulating performance agreements along with their line managers and participate in 360 degree assessment schemes. They discuss their roles and the competencies required and define objectives in conjunction with their superiors. Hence, the employees should be trained in all these activities.

Role of HR in Performance Management

The HR department today is a strategic partner and plays a vital role in pursuing a particular strategy. For facing the challenges of a globalized world, Indian organizations have reformed their HRM strategies for managing the employee performance by considering part time work, outsourcing and temporary workers. HR no longer today plays the role of a rubber stamp department, rather is a performance enabler by closely working with the to management and all the major functional departments of an organization. Companies like Maruti Udyog Ltd. and Mahindra and Mahindra, revamped their entire organizational set up and were able to create performance efficiency due to the efforts of the HR department.

Performance Development Planning & Individual Development through Performance Management

Performance management system of any organization aims at identifying the potential of development in the employees and optimally utilizing it for mutual satisfaction by providing the right support and guidance for doing well in the job. Gone are the days when performance management was simply regarded as a disciplinary and an assessment tool. Today the spectrum of performance management has widened and all its initiatives are directed towards the realization of the ultimate corporate goals. Performance development and planning is one of the most essential stages of performance management and enable establishment of performance agreement which in turn provides a framework for managing the performances throughout the year and focus on continuous improvement and individual development.

Performance and development planning is carried out jointly by the manager and the employee and in the process of discussions they both arrive at performance agreements and define performance expectations.

Performance and individual development plans are derived from an analysis of the following factors:

1. *Role Profiles:* A role profile defines a role in terms of behavioral and technical or job related

competencies. The key result areas are jointly developed by the line manager and the individual and are updated after a formal performance agreement is established. A sample role profile is illustrated in the figure below:

2. ***Objective Setting:*** Objectives are directly linked with the overall mission and vision of an organization and the work which an employee performs. Objectives cannot be dictated by the bosses rather are determined through discussions, negotiations, agreements and a compromise. Objectives help in planning for results and not only just the activities, thereby improving the overall departmental effectiveness and efficiency. An example of a performance objective could be, reduce the administrative expenses by 15% by the end of the financial year. Some of the key considerations for developing performance objectives are:

   · Define short term goals which may generate long term gains.

- Identify the possible obstacles and the complex issues in the process of realization of these objectives.

- Create flexibility into the system so that necessary changes can be added as and when required.

- Keep a track of the resource needs.

3. *Performance measures and assessment:* The performance assessments summarize the contributions of an employee over the entire period of assessment. The major goal of a performance assessment is to recognize the degree to which an employee successfully delivered his performance and the extent to which the standards and objectives were achieved.

4. *Performance planning:* Performance plans are an outcome of joint agreement between the individual and the line manager regarding what they are expected to do and know and how they are expected to behave for realizing the role objectives. These can

be also regarded as work plans set for achieving targets and meeting the project deadlines.

5. ***Development planning:*** A personal development plan is a learning action plan which is formulated with the support of the manager and the organization which may take the form of a formal training, coaching, mentoring, job enrichment, project work and job enlargement. The plan aims at adhering to the requirements of the policy of continuous development and developing the potential of individuals for higher positions.

6. ***The performance agreement:*** performance agreements define the corporate core values, objectives, role requirements, performance measures, knowledge, skills and abilities, a performance plan and an individual's development plan.

Performance Improvement Programs and Their Implications for Organizations

What are PIPs (Performance Improvement Plans/Programs)?

This one deals with a rather sad aspect of contemporary organizational policies, yet this is an important aspect that affects all employees and the HR function in addition to the line managers. We often hear the term involuntary separation, which means the resignation of employees after being asked to put in their papers. This happens either because the employee has not performed even to the lowest bar or standard or because the employee would have broken some cardinal rule of the organization. We shall be focusing on the first aspect in this discussion.

Performance improvement plans or programs are monitored, structured, and result based activities wherein employees who are performing below the average demanded by the organization are expected to do better under the PIP, which is when the line managers in conjunction with the HR managers monitor the performance of the employees. Though this is an undesirable situation for the employees to find themselves in a PIP, it is a fact of life that organizations implement these PIPs for employees at all levels.

The Performance Improvement Plans/Programs (PIP) Process and the Roles of the Stakeholders

The placement of the employee in a PIP takes place after due consultation between the employee, the manager, and the HR manager. In many cases, employees are placed on watch without the PIP if their performance is deemed unsatisfactory. Often, employees are observed for two consecutive performance cycles and if their performance does not improve or worsens, then the decision to place the employee under PIP are taken. Many line managers are reluctant to go for PIPs straightway as once the employee is placed in a PIP; his or her performance is monitored not only by the line manager but also by the HR manager. This means that each deliverable that the employee completes is checked for compliance with the performance standards by both the line manager and the HR manager who though does not get involved in the technicalities and subject matter, nonetheless asks for status reports from the manager and the employee. Indeed, many organizations view the PIPs as a waste of time of all stakeholders as dramatic improvements in performance are unlikely going by the statistics. On the other hand, organizations need a valid reason to terminate the services of employees and hence, the PIPs are designed to motivate the employee and set stern conditions for him or her so that their performance improves.

PIP and its Effect on Employees

From the employee's perspective, PIPs are like an insult as the very basis of their work is being challenged. Many employees usually take the hint when placed on PIP or if the manager indicates such a course of action to them and resign so that the embarrassment is saved for everybody. Indeed, it is a rather sad state of affairs if even after the PIP the employee does not ramp up on his or her performance. Of course, not all PIPs end up this way and there are many success stories shared by managers about how employees did improve their performance after being placed in the PIP. Whatever be the outcome, the mere mention of the PIP is by itself an indication that the organization has lost trust in the employee. Further, the issue of personal bias enters the scene as well as some managers would like to settle scores with the employees whom they do not like for whatever reason and hence, they insist on PIPs for those employees. It needs to be remembered that this is not a common occurrence as there are many checks and balances in the organizational structure that are explicitly designed to prevent such an occurrence.

Closing Thoughts

Finally, in these economically challenging times, employees are putting in their best efforts as neither do they want themselves to be under PIPs or they try other companies because the shrinking job market has reduced the opportunities available to the employees.

Performance Management and Reward Practices

Today organizations are showing a high degree of commitment towards reinforcement of reward practices which are aligned with other HR practices and the goals of the organization for attracting, retaining and motivating employees. Efficient reward practices helps in attracting result driven professionals who can thrive and succeed in performance based environments. Hence, it is a crucial motivator and may contribute towards the enhancement of the productivity of the employees if implemented properly. For example, *Continental Airlines* as a part of their turnaround strategy introduced on time bonus incentive package according to which an employee will gain a bonus of $65 every month for ensuring on time flight operations.

An effective reward system should be linked with the performance development system, which focuses on performance based pay and offers ample learning opportunities along with a healthy work environment. Variable pay can play a crucial role in boosting the performance of the employees especially the star performers instead of the fixed pay packages. Few such reward practices may take the forms of gain sharing, bonuses, team based incentives, profit sharing, ESOP's and equity based incentive awards.

An efficient management of reward system may have a beneficial effect upon the performance in several ways - instilling a sense of ownership amongst the employees, may facilitate long term focus with continuous improvement, reduces service operating costs, promotes team work, minimizes employee dissatisfaction and enhanced employee interest in the financial performance of the company. Few organizations like General Mills, reward their employees for attaining new skills which may add value to the organizational performance and thereby facilitate job rotation, cross training and self managed work teams. Few organizations also recognize exceptional performance by providing recognition awards and lump-sum merit awards for winning employee commitment and attaining long term beneficial results. Example, TISCO, offers instant or on the spot rewards, monthly rewards and annual rewards to its employees under its 'Shabashi scheme'.

A healthy pay for performance strategy should incorporate the following components as is provided in the table given below:

Pay for Performance Strategy		
Category	*Performance Measures*	*Basis for Rewards*
Corporate Leaders	BSC, shareholders returns and EVA	Employee stock ownership and profit sharing.
Business Unit Leaders	Profitability of the unit	Results Sharing.
Functional Leaders	Level of contribution towards the corporate goals	Milestone Awards
General Employees	Specific KRA's achieved measured periodically	Profit/gain sharing, bonuses
Source: Sullivan E (1999), "Moving to a pay for performance strategy: Lessons from the Trenches",		

> ## *In Risher, H(Ed.), Aligning Pay and Results, AMACOM:NY.*

Today, variable pay is a very vital component in the reward practices of an organization and it differs across various sectors also. A table given below presents the trends in the usage of variable pay component across different sectors in two different years:

Sector	*2001 (Variable pay in %)*	*2005 (Variable pay in %)*
Financial Services	19.2	23.5
Telecommunications	14	17.8
ITES	12.9	16.4
IT	10.9	13.7
Banking	13.5	23.2
Manufacturing	11	16.2
FMCG	13.3	16.5

Rewards can be a vital source of motivation for the employees but only if it is administered under right conditions. Few strategies which improve the effectiveness of rewards are given below:

- Linking rewards with the performance
- Implement team rewards for the interdependent jobs for example Xerox.
- Ensuring that the rewards are relevant. Example Wal-Mart, rewards bonuses to the top executives which is based on the company's overall performance whereas the frontline employees earn bonus on the basis of the sales figure or targets attained by their store.
- Ensuring that the rewards are valued by the employees.
- Checking out for the undesirable consequences of administration of any reward practice.

Besides the monetary rewards, the contemporary employees desire for non monetary rewards which may be in the form of better career opportunities, skills development and recognition programs. Many IT and project based organizations give much importance to non-monetary rewards for maximizing employee satisfaction.

Job Design Practices and Performance Management

An organization's performance largely depends upon the HRM practices of which one of the major components is the job design practices. Organizations like Imation, Xerox, etc, motivate their employees by designing challenging and interesting jobs. Job designing is the process of assigning tasks to a particular job by equally considering the interdependency of those tasks with the other jobs. Job design practices can influence the work motivation and the performance of the employees by increasing the work efficiency through job specialization. These practices have evolved and are in a state of constant change due to the changes in the business environment, increased role of information technology, workforce flexibility and technological changes.

The *Job Characteristics Model* suggests a framework of how effective job design practices can lead to improved work motivation and satisfaction of employees thereby leading to improved organizational performance.

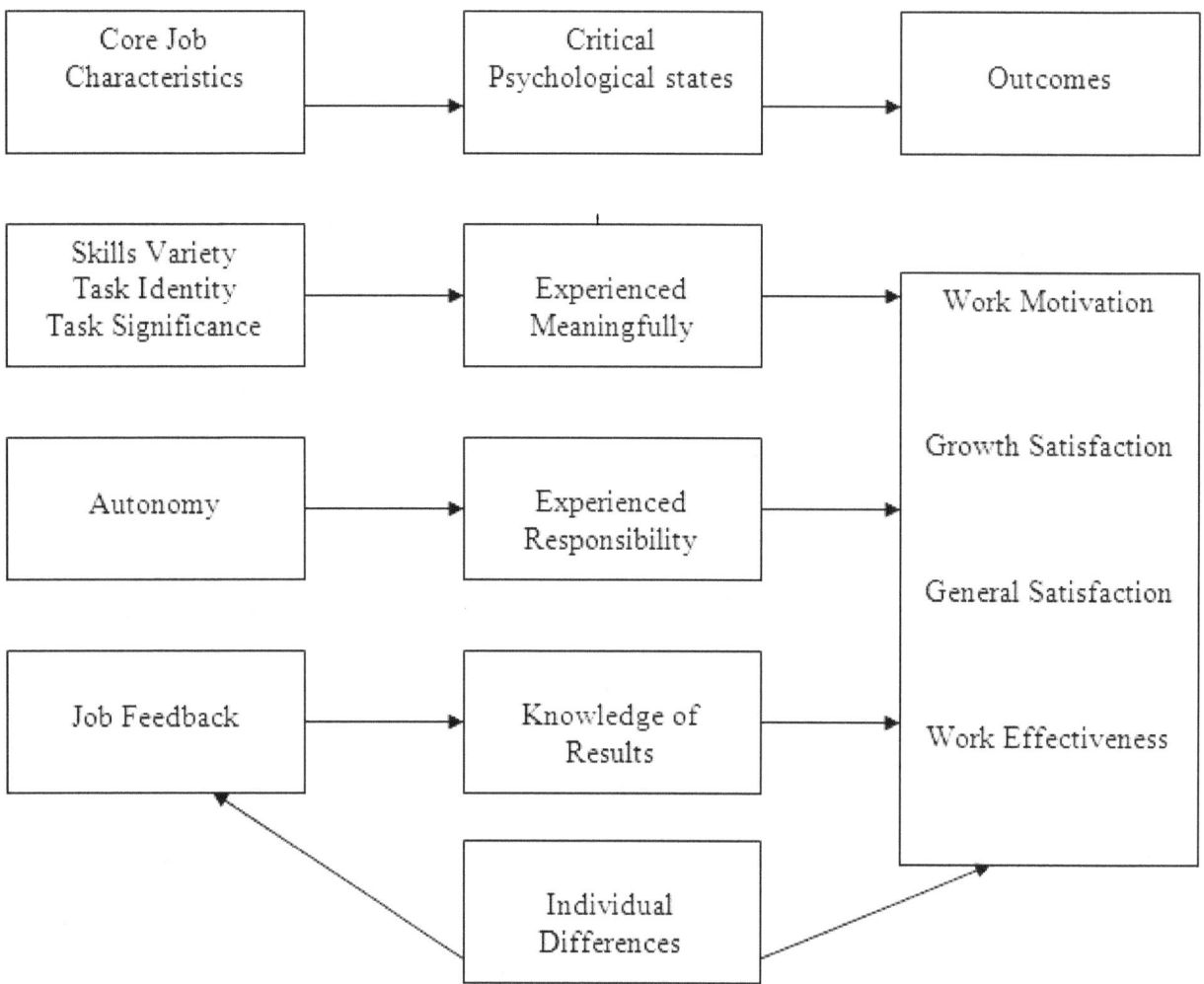

Source: Work Redesign by J.R. Hackman and G.Oldham

According to the job characteristics model, employees will remain motivated and satisfied if the jobs satisfy the following characteristics:

1. ***Skill Variety:*** Refers to the extent to which the employees use different skills and talents for performing different tasks for fulfilling the requirements of a job.

2. ***Task Identity:*** Refers to the extent to which a job can be completed as a whole or can be completed in identifiable piece of work.

3. ***Task Significance:*** Refers to the degree to which a job has an impact on the organization or on the society.

4. ***Autonomy:*** Jobs having a high degree of autonomy offer tremendous freedom in fulfilling the task requirements.

5. ***Job Feedback:*** Refers to the extent to which the employees provide a feedback about how well are they performing their jobs based on their experiences in the job.

Job design need not necessarily increase the work motivation of the employees as it is affected by the individual differences. Factors such as employee competence, their satisfaction with their work environment and their growth needs influence the motivation level of the employees.

Job design strategies which improve work motivation:

1. *Job Rotation:* It is a form of job design practice in which the employees are moved from one job to another. Job rotation helps in reducing job boredom and help in developing a flexible workforce. Job rotation creates multi skilled employees.

2. *Job Enlargement:* It is about increasing the number of tasks in a job for an employee. It helps in improving work efficiency and flexibility.

3. *Job Enrichment:* It occurs when the employees are entrusted with additional responsibilities for scheduling, coordinating and planning their own work.

4. *Alternative Work Schedule options:* Designing work schedule according to the convenience of the employees so that they can balance their work time and personal time. These may be in the form of:

- *Compressed work weeks:* This implies reducing the number of working days by keeping the number of hours of work the same.

- *Shorter workweek:* This means reducing the working hours per week, say from 40 hours to 35 hours.

- *Flexitime:* Allowing employees with flexible scheduling options wherein they decide their arrival and departure time from their organization.

- *Telecommuting:* Allows the employee to perform their jobs through computers which is linked with their offices.

Leadership Development and Performance Management

Leadership Development in the present century has become a buzzword and many organizations use this as a crucial tool for gaining a competitive advantage in the business. Developing leadership talent is one of the most crucial functions of performance management today, as the system has evolved from an evaluative to a developmental and result driven framework. *The inputs from the personal development plans, performance appraisals, and competency frameworks provide necessary information for identifying the top leadership talent in an organization*.

According to the survey findings of Ninth House Co., Jan 2006, about 90% of leading organizations integrate their leadership development programmes with performance management and succession planning. The same survey results also reveal that about 95% of the respondents appoint external executive coaches for conducting leadership development programmes and almost 85% deploy 360 degree feedback tools. The survey results prove that different organizations adopt multidimensional approaches towards leadership development by utilizing a variety of learning techniques which is again dependent upon the levels of management.

Leadership development is an integrative framework and is interconnected with the other processes of an organization. In the opinion of Raelin (2004), leadership development should be integrated with the major organizational strategies, culture and the other crucial processes and sub processes for attaining the predetermined objectives. Today organizations, pay a heavy importance to the measurement of return on investment (ROI) subsequent to the implementation of any leadership development programme in terms of improvements in current performance and of the future as well (Kincaid and Gordick, 2003). Organizations like Pepsi Co., Johnson and Johnson and many others have introduced newer modalities for measuring the benefits of leadership development efforts in quantifiable terms.

Organizations today use a plethora of assessment tools to identify and develop the individual talents and the talent pool for successfully meeting their current people requirements and for their future. The Competency model has proven to be one of the most effective tools as it uses performance matrix, promotability matrix and multi rater 360 degree feedback tools for gathering information on the organizational talent pool. For example, Mc Kinsey recommended a three tier system for sorting the talent base in an organization. The ones in the top group are deployed in a fast track to leadership in terms of both responsibilities and compensation. The ones in the middle group are encouraged to progress towards the future group of leadership whereas those in the bottom are pressurized or forced to either "shape up" or "ship out". Some of the most commonly used techniques adopted by the contemporary organizations in the leadership programmes are mentoring, <u>360 degree feedback</u>, project assignments, <u>job rotations</u>, team assignments, on the job training, coaching, etc.

According to the latest survey findings from Fortune (September, 2007) on top companies for leaders, most of the organizations offer internal training to their executives for grooming future leaders. Some of the crucial findings of the survey report of fortune are provided below:

- Many reputed companies prefer to invest their major time and money on leadership for gaining a competitive advantage. For example, in Mc Donald's the CEO personally reviews the top 200 managers and similarly at GE, the top 600 managers' performances are reviewed by the CEO. GE spends heavily upon the leadership development programmes by representing the high potential employees to Crotonville, New York, leadership development center.

- Organizations like Whirlpool and Natura Cosmeticos, stress on consistent feedback and support through mentoring and coaching in the leadership development process.

- Organizations like GE and Nokia aim at developing teams instead of just the individuals. Nokia adopts a Finnish culture which focuses upon leadership instead of just the leaders. Similarly, P&G runs inspirational leadership development programmes for inspiring leaders at the top.

Leadership development process today has evolved as a facilitative and a strategic process aiming at improving the organizational and individual performance by identifying and developing the leadership talent in a planned and integrated manner.

Performance Reviews - Its Objectives and Criterions

Review of performance once or twice in a year provides an objective or a sense of focus on the key performance or development issues. Performance review meetings form the basis for enabling both the managers and the individuals to positively explore ways for improving the performance in the near future and to identify solutions for resolving the issues which come in the way of attainment of predetermined performance standards.

Some of the crucial *objectives of performance reviews are as follows:*

- Performance planning
- Employee motivation and empowerment
- Learning and Development
- Acts as a two way channel for communication for discussing the roles, expectations, relationships and work problems.

Performance review meetings should focus on two major areas: Firstly on *performance improvement measures* and secondly, the *meeting should be forward looking* in nature rather than backward looking. The main problems which normally arise during the period of performance reviews are:

- Identification of performance measures and the criterions for evaluating performance.
- Problems in collection of genuine performance related evidences.
- Manager's bias.
- Conflicts between the reviewers and the people being reviewed.
- Defensive behavior from the people under review as a response to some criticisms.

The above discussed problems can be checked by adopting the following measures:

- Ensuring that the criterions for evaluating performance covers the mutually agreed quantifiable objectives, competencies based on role analysis and properly laid performance standards.
- Monitor performance on a continuous basis throughout the year against the agreed objectives,

behavioral dimensions and the performance standards.

- Adopt measures to minimize bias.
- Train managers in building positivism in the entire process and in providing constructive criticism and feedback.
- Briefing the people involved in the process regarding the benefits from this process to both the parties for reducing the defensive behaviors on the part of the employees under review.

The golden rules for conducting a performance review meeting:

- Managers should be prepared by referring to a list of objectives and their notes on performance throughout the year.
- Sufficient time should be provided for allowing a full discussion.
- Building a friendly, supportive and an informal environment.
- Providing a constructive feedback.

- Use Time productively and constructively.
- Praises should be used by the managers for some special achievements.
- The individuals should be allowed to do most of the talking.
- Self Assessments should be invited.
- Only performance related issues should be discussed and not the personality.
- Analysis of performance should be encouraged.
- End the review meeting on a positive note agreeing upon measurable objectives and a plan of action.

Guiding principles of a review meeting:

- Achievements should be discussed in relation with the objectives and the performance development plans.
- Assess the level of competence achieved by the individual which is defined in their roles.
- Assess the extent to which the individual's behavior is in accordance with the organizational values.

- Identify the problems involved in the achievement of objectives or the performance standards and also establish the reasons for such problems.

- Discuss about the individual's working relationships with his/her managers, colleagues and also the subordinates.

- Develop agreeable actions for resolving those problems.

- Review and revise performance standards if required.

- Develop a personal development plan and agree upon a performance plan for the next review period.

Absenteeism at Work and its Implications for Organizational Performance

Absenteeism and its Perils

Absenteeism or taking leave from work is a growing problem for many organizations that have to deal with the loss of employee time and productivity which then result in decreased earnings and revenues for these organizations. While legitimate leave of absence from work is usually taken as the norm and is indeed sanctioned in the form of annual leave and holidays apart from sick leave, in recent years, employees in many organizations have begun to take extended breaks from work be it for personal or health or any other reasons. It is not the case here that employees must not take leave of absence. Rather, the contention of this discussion is that prolonged and unnecessary leave of absence as well as unplanned and disruptive leave of absences must be regulated if the organizations have to remain profitable and at the same time, the employees put in their best at work.

In other words, if the employees stick to planned leave of absence and take sick leaves only in genuine cases, then there should not be a problem with the balance between organizational needs and personal needs. However, when employees go on leave suddenly and in the middle of important projects where the deliverables are of utmost importance, it is certainly the case that the organization suffers as a result of this.

Authorized and Unauthorized Leaves

The previous section dealt with the pros and cons of planned and unplanned leaves. If we now turn to authorized and unauthorized leaves of absence, we find that once an employee decides to absent himself or herself without informing his or her manager or supervisor, then he or she can be slotted as gone AWOL or Absent Without Official Leave which is a term that was first used in the armed forces and is now widely used in Human Resource parlance to denote those employees who have absented themselves without notice. Indeed, contemporary organizations and the HR personnel are not taking kindly these instances as well as the managers who often report such instances and mention it in the employees' appraisal to indicate a serious breach of discipline. The point here is that when employees absent themselves suddenly and without authorization, the managers have to reallocate their work and find other employees to complete their tasks.

Apart from this, the managers might not be completely in the loop about the specific tasks being done by the employee who has absented himself or herself without authorization. This is because in the laissez faire work environment of the 21st century, often it is not possible for the managers to have minute details of what an employee is working on. Moreover, when employees absent themselves suddenly, the other employees might be having their hands full and hence, it might not be possible to reallocate the tasks completely.

Absent Without Leave or AWOL

Absenteeism takes on a more dangerous turn when employees go AWOL and engage in suspicious and illegal activities which can have a bearing on the organizations as the individual in question is a part of the organization and hence, the organization bears some responsibility towards his or her actions. This is the reason why many organizations in recent years have come out with strict policies and rules and regulations that specify an outer limit for the number of days an employee can go AWOL without informing his or her manager. In some multinationals like Fidelity, this is as short as two days because the reasoning is that in this connected and mobile age, the employee or his or her family as well as friends can contact the organization within two days if the employee is absent because of legitimate reasons like being involved in an accident, or having a personal emergency.

Further, organizations like IBM and Microsoft have call trees that can be activated in case of emergencies and procedures to activate continuity of business routines. This means that the employees have to give alternate contact numbers to their managers in the call trees so that the employee and the alternate contact can be reached in case of any serious event because of which the employee is unable to reach the manager.

Absenteeism from Trainings and Events

We have so far focused on absenteeism from work and its consequences for organizational performance. If we consider absenteeism from trainings and important events like Annual Days, All Hands Meets, and Town Halls with the senior leadership, we find that many organizations are frowning on this kind of absenteeism as well. The contention here is that for smoother organizational communication, employees have to necessarily attend these meets and hence, absenteeism is not being tolerated here. moreover, being absent from trainings entails monetary losses for organizations as training nowadays is an expensive affair and is usually priced on a per seat basis.

Further, finding replacements at the last minute is tough for many organizations and hence, many HR managers and direct managers often make it a point to mention absenteeism from training in the overall performance assessments of the employees. Before concluding this discussion, it would be pertinent to point that a balanced and objective look at absenteeism would reveal the fact that in most cases, there are legitimate reasons on both sides i.e. the employees and the organizations. Therefore, the concluding statement is that both employees and the organizations should realize their responsibilities and conduct themselves in a manner that does not lead to legal and other complications for either side.

www.ingramcontent.com/pod-product-compliance
Lightning Source LLC
Chambersburg PA
CBHW080826180526
45168CB00006B/2589